101 FACTS

ABOUT

TATE McRAE

Coloring, Quizzes, Journaling, and More!

Meet Tate McRae

Tate McRae was born on July 1, 2003, in Calgary, Alberta, Canada. From an early age, she was immersed in the arts, thanks to her mother, a dance instructor.

Tate first gained widespread recognition as a standout contestant on "So You Think You Can Dance" at just 13 years old, where she showcased her incredible talent and passion for performing.

Despite her roots in dance, Tate's passion for music soon took center stage, and she began sharing her original songs on YouTube, paving the way for her successful music career.

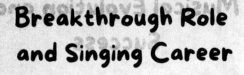

Breakthrough Role and Singing Career

Tate McRae's breakthrough role came as a finalist on "So You Think You Can Dance" at 13, showcasing her remarkable dance skills. She then transitioned to music, gaining international acclaim with her hit single "you broke me first." The song's raw emotion and catchy melody propelled her singing career forward, highlighting her distinctive voice and introspective songwriting. Tate's unique artistry has quickly established her as a rising star in the pop music scene.

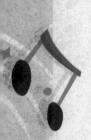

Musical Evolution and Success

Tate McRae's musical evolution is marked by her transition from dance to a dynamic singing career. Starting with the emotionally charged "you broke me first," she established herself with a distinctive sound blending pop and introspective lyrics. Her subsequent releases, including tracks like "she's all i wanna be," demonstrate her growth as an artist and her ability to connect deeply with listeners. Tate's success continues to build, with each new release showcasing her evolving talent and solidifying her place in pop music.

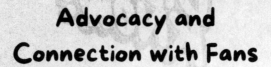

Advocacy and Connection with Fans

Tate McRae is not only known for her music but also for her strong connection with fans and advocacy for mental health. Through her lyrics and public statements, she addresses themes of self-empowerment and personal struggle, resonating deeply with her audience. Tate actively engages with her fans on social media, offering support and fostering a sense of community. Her openness about her own challenges and her genuine interactions have endeared her to many, making her a relatable and influential figure.

- She has Scottish and German ancestry.

- She has an older brother named Tucker.

- Her father is a lawyer, and her mother is a dance instructor.

- She Began dancing at the age of six.

- She started at her mother's dance studio in Calgary.

- She received ballet training at The School of Alberta Ballet.

- She lived in Oman for three years due to her father's work.

- She speaks English and some Arabic.

"So You Think You Can Dance" A Stardom Start

Tate McRae's stardom began as a finalist on So You Think You Can Dance at just 13, where she impressed audiences with her exceptional dance talent. Her transition to music was marked by the release of her debut single "you broke me first," which quickly gained popularity and established her as a rising star. This breakout hit highlighted her unique voice and emotional depth, propelling her into the spotlight and setting the stage for a successful music career.

The Impact of Dance on her Career

Tate McRae's dance talent significantly impacted her career, providing a strong foundation for her subsequent musical success. Her early exposure on So You Think You Can Dance showcased her exceptional skills and versatility, earning her widespread recognition and a dedicated fan base. This background in dance not only highlighted her artistic range but also contributed to her stage presence and performance style in music. Her dance experience adds depth to her artistry, enriching her musical expression and captivating audiences.

On Stage and Behind the Scenes

On "So You Think You Can Dance", Tate McRae's presence was magnetic both on stage and behind the scenes. On stage, she dazzled with her exceptional dance technique and emotional performances, impressing judges and viewers with her versatility and artistry. Behind the scenes, her dedication and professionalism were evident as she navigated the intense competition with grace and resilience. Tate's time on the show not only showcased her talent but also set the stage for her future success in the entertainment industry.

Musical Contributions

Tate McRae's musical contributions are marked by her distinctive voice and emotionally resonant lyrics. Her debut single "you broke me first" captured global attention with its raw, introspective take on heartbreak. Following this, she released tracks like "she's all i wanna be" and "GOLD," each showcasing her ability to blend catchy melodies with deep, personal themes. Tate's songwriting often reflects themes of self-discovery and resilience, adding a fresh perspective to contemporary pop music. Her innovative approach continues to shape her growing impact on the genre.

Moving Forward

Tate McRae is poised to build on her already impressive career with new musical explorations and creative ventures. Her growth as an artist suggests a commitment to evolving her sound while staying true to her authentic voice. Fans can anticipate fresh releases that push boundaries and delve deeper into personal and universal themes. With her strong foundation and artistic vision, Tate is set to make an even greater impact on the music industry, continually expanding her influence and reaching new heights.

- She became the first Canadian finalist on the U.S. version of So You Think You Can Dance in 2016.
- She is known for her contemporary dance style.
- She won numerous dance competitions, including the Mini Best Dancer title at The Dance Awards in 2013.
- She started her YouTube channel in 2011, where she posted dance videos and vlogs.

Activity: Stories in Sound

Tate McRae's music skillfully blends raw emotion with compelling storytelling. Her songs, like "you broke me first" and "she's all i wanna be," transform personal experiences into relatable narratives, capturing a wide range of human emotions.

McRae's ability to convey introspective themes and subtle feelings through her music highlights her exceptional talent as a songwriter and performer. Her tracks resonate deeply with listeners, making her work both impactful and profoundly engaging.

"You Broke Me First."

Story Behind the Song:

"You Broke Me First" by Tate McRae is an empowering anthem about moving on from a past relationship. It captures her assertive response to an ex's attempt to reconnect, blending confidence with catchy beats.

Activity:

Reflect on a past relationship or experience that significantly impacted you. Write a short paragraph about how it shaped your personal growth and what you learned from it. Then, craft a four-line chorus that encapsulates the journey of embracing the lessons and moving forward with a sense of empowerment and self-love.

Date:

"One Day"

Story Behind the Song:

Tate McRae's song "One Day" reflects her feelings of longing and hope for the future. Inspired by personal experiences, it captures the bittersweet anticipation of a brighter tomorrow despite current challenges.

Activity:

Reflect on a time when you felt unsure about pursuing a new creative venture. Write a brief paragraph about how you navigated these doubts and found the courage to embrace this new challenge. Then, compose a four-line verse that captures the essence of overcoming self-doubt and celebrating your newfound confidence in exploring new horizons.

"One Day"

Story Behind the Song:
Tate McRae's song "One Day" reflects her feelings of longing and hope for the future. Inspired by personal experiences, it captures the bittersweet anticipation of a brighter tomorrow despite current challenges.

Activity:
Reflect on a time when you felt unsure about pursuing a new creative venture. Write a brief paragraph about how you navigated these doubts and found the courage to embrace this new challenge. Then, compose a four-line verse that captures the essence of overcoming self-doubt and celebrating your newfound confidence in exploring new horizons.

"Gold"

Story Behind the Song:

"Gold" by Tate McRae reflects her journey to self-empowerment and confidence. Inspired by overcoming self-doubt, the song uses gold as a metaphor for inner strength and worth, celebrating personal resilience and self-affirmation.

Activity:

Reflect on a time when you faced a challenge and found the strength to stay positive. Write a brief paragraph about how you overcame it and what you learned. Then, craft a four-line verse that captures your journey of resilience and renewed optimism, inspired by the song's message of inner strength and self-worth.

"Gold"

Date:

Story Behind the Song:
"Gold" by Tate McRae reflects her journey to self-empowerment and confidence. Inspired by overcoming self-doubt, the song uses gold as a metaphor for inner strength and worth, celebrating personal resilience and self-affirmation.

Activity:
Reflect on a time when you faced a challenge and found the strength to stay positive. Write a brief paragraph about how you overcame it and what you learned. Then, craft a four-line verse that captures your journey of resilience and renewed optimism, inspired by the song's message of inner strength and self-worth.

Date:

- She cites choreographers like Mia Michaels and Travis Wall as inspirations.
- Tate McRae worked with several high-profile choreographers, including Brian Friedman.
- She has appeared as a dancer in several music videos for artists like Justin Bieber.
- She wrote her first song at the age of 13.
- She is inspired by personal experiences and emotions.
- Her song "One Day" was uploaded to her YouTube channel in 2017.

- She cites choreographers like Mia Michaels and Travis Wall as inspirations.
- Tate McRae worked with several high-profile choreographers, including Brian Friedman.
- She has appeared as a dancer in several music videos for artists like Justin Bieber.
- She wrote her first song at the age of 13.
- She is inspired by personal experiences and emotions.
- Her song "One Day" was uploaded to her YouTube channel in 2017.

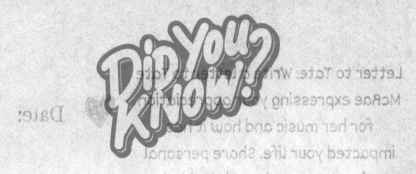

- Tate McRae often starts with melodies before developing lyrics.
- She is influenced by artists like Billie Eilish, Khalid, and Post Malone.
- Her song "One Day" went viral on YouTube, gaining millions of views.
- Tate McRae signed with RCA Records in 2019.
- She released her debut single "Tear Myself Apart" in 2019.
- She released her debut EP, All the Things I Never Said, in January 2020.

Letter to Tate: Write a letter to Tate McRae expressing your appreciation for her music and how it has impacted your life. Share personal stories or memories related to her songs.

Date:

- Her song "You Broke Me First" became a global hit in 2020.

- Her song "You Broke Me First" has over a billion streams on Spotify.

- The song charted in the top 20 in multiple countries, including the UK and the US.

- Her second EP, Too Young to Be Sad, was released in 2021.

- Tate McRae released her debut album I Used to Think I Could Fly in May 2022.

DID YOU KNOW?

- Tate McRae often writes about heartbreak, self-reflection, and the struggles of youth.
- Tate McRae has collaborated with artists like Troye Sivan, Khalid, and Lil Mosey.
- She is often involved in the creative direction of her music videos.
- She embarked on her first headlining tour in 2022.
- She is known for incorporating dance into her live performances.

1. What is the central theme of Tate McRae's song "Gold"?

A. Romance and heartbreak

B. Overcoming obstacles and self-worth

C. Friendship and loyalty

D. Adventure and discovery

2. Which song helped Tate McRae gain significant recognition in her early music career?

A. "Gold"

B. "you broke me first"

C. "she's all I wanna be"

D. "Starlight"

3. What metaphor does Tate McRae use in "Gold" to symbolize inner strength and self-worth?

A. Diamonds

B. Silver

C. Bronze

D. Gold

1. What is the central theme of Tate McRae's song "Gold"?

A.
B. Overcoming obstacles and self-worth
D. Adventure and discovery

B. "You broke me first"
C. "she's all I wanna be"
D. "greedy"

3. W
inner strength and self-worth?

A. Diamonds
B. silver
C. Bronze
D. Gold

2. D) Gold
2. B) "you broke me first"
self-worth
1. B) Overcoming obstacles and
Answers:

- She has performed at major award shows, including the MTV Europe Music Awards.

- She has appeared on shows like The Tonight Show Starring Jimmy Fallon and Jimmy Kimmel Live!

- Tate McRae was nominated for several iHeartRadio Music Awards.

- She was nominated for Best New Artist in the MTV Video Music Awards in 2021.

- She was nominated for Breakthrough Artist of the Year in the Juno Awards in 2021.
- Tate McRae was nominated for Choice Music Web Star in the Teen Choice Awards in 2020.
- She has received nominations at the Canadian Music Awards.
- Tate McRae is one of the youngest artists to surpass a billion streams on Spotify.

> "MUSIC HAS ALWAYS BEEN MY OUTLET. IT'S THE WAY I EXPRESS MY FEELINGS AND CONNECT WITH OTHERS."

- Tate McRae

Did You Know?

- Tate McRae was featured as an Up Next artist on Apple Music.
- She enjoys eating sushi.
- Her favorite color is purple.
- She has a pet dog.
- She is known for her casual and edgy style.
- Tate McRae is active on platforms like Instagram, Twitter, and TikTok.
- She is open about her struggles with anxiety and mental health.

- Tate McRae is involved in charitable initiatives, particularly those supporting mental health.
- She looks up to artists like Adele and Rihanna.
- She enjoys watching romantic comedies.
- She likes painting and drawing in her free time.
- Tate McRae loves traveling and has visited several countries for work and leisure.

Inspired by Tate: Tate McRae inspires people with her music. Write about something you've done that you feel proud of, inspired by Tate's messages of kindness and confidence.

Date:

_____

_____

_____

_____

_____

_____

_____

_____

_____

_____

_____

_____

_____

1. Which TV show did Tate McRae first gain fame from?

A. America's Got Talent

B. The Voice

C. So You Think You Can Dance

D. Dancing with the Stars

2. What year was Tate McRae's single "you broke me first" released?

A. 2019

B. 2020

C. 2021

D. 2022

3. What is the focus of the lyrics in Tate McRae's song "she's all I wanna be"?

A. Celebrating personal achievements

B. self-doubt and comparison

C. Falling in love

D. Overcoming a breakup

Answers:

1. C) So You Think You Can Dance

2. B) 2020

3. B) self-doubt and comparison

1. Which TV show did Tate McRae first gain fame from?

   A. America's Got Talent

   B. The Voice

   C. So You Think You Can Dance

   D. Dancing with the Stars

2. What year was Tate McRae's single "you broke me first" released?

   A. 2019

   B. 2020

   C. 2021

   D. 2022

3. What is the focus of the lyrics in Tate McRae's song "she's all I wanna be"?

   A. Celebrating personal achievements

   B. Self-doubt and comparison

   C. Falling in love

   D. Overcoming a breakup

Answers:
1. C) So You Think You Can Dance
2. B) 2020
3. B) Self-doubt and comparison

Did You Know?

- Tate McRae enjoys playing soccer.
- She is close friends with fellow artists like Olivia Rodrigo.
- She is known for her expressive and fluid dance movements.
- One of her favorite songs to perform is "You Broke Me First."
- Tate McRae attended her first concert at age 10.
- She plays the piano.
- She enjoys reading The Fault in Our Stars by John Green.

- She loves watching Friends.
- She enjoys spending time by the beach.
- She is a Cancer.
- Tate McRae hopes to collaborate with Billie Eilish someday.
- She lives by the motto "Stay true to yourself."
- She has a passion for visual arts and sketching.
- Tate McRae loves doing pirouettes
- She has a small tattoo on her wrist.

"

"I THINK SONGWRITING
IS SUCH A PERSONAL
EXPERIENCE. IT'S
ALMOST LIKE WRITING
A DIARY THAT
EVERYONE CAN READ."

- Tate McRae

Did You Know?

- She loves Christmas.
- Tate McRae worked as a dance teacher before her music career took off.
- Tate McRae is one of the youngest artists to achieve global success.
- Her YouTube channel has millions of subscribers.
- She has millions of followers on Instagram and TikTok.
- She was nominated on Billboard's 21 Under 21 list.
- She was featured on Forbes' 30 Under 30 list in music.

- She was highlighted as an artist to watch by Rolling Stone.
- Tate McRae is one of the most streamed female artists on Spotify.
- She topped Apple Music charts globally.
- She has performed in multiple countries, including the US, UK, and Australia.
- Tate McRae has performed at major festivals like Lollapalooza and Coachella.
- She is working on her second studio album.

QUIZ TIME!!!!

• she was highlighted as an artist to
watch by Rolling stone.

1. What was Tate McRae's role in the music video for "you broke me first"?

streamed female artists on spotify.

• She topped Apple Music charts
globally.

• she has performed in multiple
countries, including the us, UK, and

    A. Choreographer

    B. Director

    C. Lead performer

    D. Producer

2. Which of the following songs is NOT by Tate McRae?

    A. "you broke me first"

    B. "GOLD"

    C. "drivers license"

    D. "she's all I wanna be"

3. What is the primary genre of Tate McRae's music?

    A. Rock

she is working on her second studio
album.

    B. Country

    C. Pop

    D. Jazz

- She is interested in exploring acting opportunities.
- Tate McRae plans to release a documentary about her life and career.
- She has launched her own line of merchandise.
- She has collaborated with brands like Nike and Reebok.
- Tate McRae plans to launch her own fashion line.
- She is interested in writing a book about her experiences.
- She aspires to compose music for films.

- She wants to start her own charity foundation focused on mental health.
- Tate McRae is interested in voice acting for animated films.
- She is passionate about environmental issues and sustainability.
- She wants to explore music production and producing for other artists.
- Tate McRae aims to become an inspirational speaker for young people.

"

"I WANT MY MUSIC TO BE HONEST AND REAL. I WANT PEOPLE TO RELATE TO IT AND FEEL SOMETHING."

- Tate McRae

- She aspires to use her platform for global change.

- Tate McRae hopes to have a long and impactful career in the music industry.

- Tate McRae draws inspiration from her personal experiences, relationships, and observations of the world around her.

- Her first dance routine was a ballet performance at a local recital.

- Tate McRae is her real name; she does not use a stage name.

- She has won several national dance titles before transitioning to music.

- Known for her unique and trendsetting fashion sense, she often collaborates with stylists and designers.

- Tate McRae has become an influential figure for many young aspiring musicians and dancers.

WORD SEARCH

Tate McRae is her real name; she does

not use a stage name.

She has won several national dance

titles before transitioning to music.

Known for her unique and

trendsetting fashion sense, she often

collaborates with stylists and

designers.

Tate McRae has become an influential

figure for many young aspiring

musicians and dancers.

```
P S E Q S C C A D T B E
A T A N R Q P A C S Q N
S Y B T E E B S H N W O
S L L O N U R P R O E I
I Q U C G Q B I I L H H
O S E W I I R R S L W S
N T U H S N O E T L E A
A M A K E U K S M I Q F
T Y O I D A E K A M F N
E H D G O S U F S O M S
```

Unique   Aspires   Fashion   Stylist
Designers   Passionate   Christmas
Millions   Broke   Blue

- Tate McRae began exploring music at a young age, writing songs and playing the piano.

- Tate McRae often writes her lyrics in a journal before turning them into full songs.

- Besides Billie Eilish, she cites artists like Taylor Swift and Ariana Grande as influences.

- Her music blends pop, alternative, and R&B genres.

- Her first music video was for "Tear Myself Apart."

DID YOU KNOW?

- Tate McRae has expressed interest in collaborating with artists across various genres, including rock and electronic music.

- Sometimes writes and produces her own music, allowing for greater creative control.

- Enjoys hiking and outdoor activities when not working.

- Regularly donates to various charitable organizations, including those supporting mental health and youth programs.

"

"I'VE LEARNED THAT IT'S OKAY TO BE VULNERABLE. IT'S ACTUALLY A STRENGTH, NOT A WEAKNESS."

- Tate McRae

Charitable Music Donates Writes Elliah
Piano Apart Tear Ballet Inspiration

WORD SEARCH

O	C	O	Z	T	D	M	C	C	T	N	O
W	R	I	T	E	S	C	I	H	Y	T	N
T	F	R	F	O	I	M	S	A	O	E	A
M	S	E	G	M	A	A	U	R	A	A	I
S	E	T	A	N	O	D	M	I	K	R	P
M	I	N	S	P	I	R	A	T	I	O	N
E	L	F	U	B	L	E	F	A	P	B	P
U	I	F	R	M	H	I	F	B	A	F	J
K	S	T	E	L	L	A	B	L	R	K	J
Y	H	T	R	A	P	A	J	E	Y	U	P

Charitable   Music   Donates   Writes   Eilish
Piano   Apart   Tear   Ballet   Inspiration

- Has been recognized with various music industry awards and honors.
- Tate McRae attended high school in Calgary before focusing on her music career.
- Advocates for mental health awareness and body positivity through her music and social media.
- Her diverse background influences her musical and artistic expressions.
- Set records for the fastest-growing song on streaming platforms upon the release of "You Broke Me First."

- Taught herself to play various musical instruments in addition to her formal training.

- Tate McRae enjoys listening to a wide range of artists, including classics like Fleetwood Mac and modern stars like Dua Lipa.

- She frequently interacts with her fans through social media and live Q&A sessions.

- Has attended major fashion shows and events, including New York Fashion Week.

Song Reflections
song that reso...
emotionally. write...
reflecting on why the song is
meaningful to you and how it makes
you feel.

Date:

1. Which song by Tate McRae is about dealing with jealousy and comparison?

    A. Feel Like S***

    B. Rubberband

    C. she's all I wanna be

    D. GOLD

2. Which of these albums features the song "you broke me first"?

    A. I used to think I could fly

    B. Only You

    C. Love and Light

    D. Untamed

3. What aspect of Tate McRae's artistry is highlighted in her song "GOLD"?

    A. Romantic relationships

    B. Personal empowerment and self-worth

    C. Travel adventures

    D. Family bonds

Answers:
1. C) she's all I wanna be
2. A) I used to think I could fly
3. B) Personal empowerment and self-worth

Song Reflections: Select a Tate McRae song that resonates with you emotionally. Write a journal entry reflecting on why the song is meaningful to you and how it makes you feel.

Date:

- Tate McRae draws inspiration from contemporary art and cinema for her music videos.
- She practices yoga and meditation to maintain physical and mental health.
- Has expressed interest in pursuing further education in music or arts.
- Took early music lessons to develop her skills in songwriting and performance.
- Shows interest in the film industry, both in acting and composing soundtracks.

- Tate McRae draws inspiration from contemporary art and cinema for her music videos.
- She practices yoga and meditation to maintain physical and mental health.
- Has expressed interest in pursuing further education in music or arts.
- Took early music lessons to develop her skills in songwriting and performance.
- Shows interest in the film industry, both in acting and composing soundtracks.

WORD SEARCH

```
Y H U I T I N D U S T R Y
M E D I T A T I O N R Y R
N F S E T A C O V D A R P
F Z I B H C I N E M A A R
I A I N E E L Y K F I N A
Z T O V A S M V O I D G C
W D C Z L Y N Y O G A E T
I U J T T U N Y I Z Y Q I
R C U Y H S C I S S A L C
W R N S Q P N E D T G C E
X E D U C A T I O N B F S
```

Education   Yoga   Practices   Health
Meditation   Cinema   Range   Classics
Advocates   Industry

- Her international travels have inspired several of her songs and music videos.
- Often engages in creative projects outside of music, including art and photography.
- She attended several prestigious music award shows, gaining recognition and experience.
- Tate McRae participates in charity events and concerts to support various causes.

"THE BEST SONGS
COME FROM REAL
EXPERIENCES AND
EMOTIONS. I TRY TO
STAY TRUE TO THAT
IN MY WRITING."

- Tate McRae

A Day In The Life Of Tate McRae !

Ever wondered what a day in the life of Tate McRae looks like? Balancing a dynamic career in music and dance. Tate's daily routine is a blend of artistry. hustle. and personal moments. Here's a peek into her world. where each day is a unique mix of creativity and dedication. shaping her path to stardom.

Morning Routine

Tate McRae's mornings start with meditation, followed by a healthy breakfast like a smoothie or avocado toast. She then warms up her voice and heads to the dance studio or gym for an energizing workout.

Finally, she reviews her schedule, checks in with her team, and sets her intentions for the day.

Studio Sessions and Songwriting

After her morning routine, Tate McRae heads to the studio, where she dives into creative work. Songwriting is deeply personal for her, often drawing from real experiences. Whether working alone or collaborating, she's focused yet open to inspiration. Balancing studio time with other commitments, Tate ensures her music remains authentic and heartfelt, pouring her emotions into every song.

Commitments

Tate McRae's schedule is packed with various commitments, from interviews and photoshoots to rehearsals and performances. Despite the demands, she prioritizes what truly matters—her music and well-being. Tate stays organized by maintaining a clear schedule, ensuring she meets deadlines without compromising her creative process. She knows when to say no, preserving time for rest and self-care. This balance allows her to stay grounded, focused, and ready to deliver her best in every aspect of her career.

Media Appearances and Interviews

Tate McRae regularly engages in media appearances with a blend of professionalism and authenticity. Whether on live TV, podcasts, or in magazine features, she remains articulate and genuine, sharing insights into her music and experiences. She balances key talking points with spontaneous moments, allowing her personality to shine and strengthening her connection with fans.

Evening Wind-Down

In the evening, Tate McRae winds down with a calming routine. She enjoys a light dinner, often something nutritious, followed by a relaxing activity like reading or watching a show. Tate then practices gentle stretching or yoga before bed, ensuring she ends the day feeling relaxed and recharged.

Discover Your Soundtrack:
List Your Top Ten "Tate McRae" Songs

On this page, jot down your top ten Tate McRae tunes. Dive into the melodies that resonate with your soul and capture your experiences. Let Tate's music be the backdrop to your journaling journey.

Discover Your Soundtrack:
Singing Journey
Listen to Top Tate McRae"
Songs

Singing Journey

Tate McRae's singing journey began in her teenage years, with her passion for music driving her from local performances to international recognition. Her unique voice and raw, emotional lyrics quickly set her apart. Through dedication and hard work, she has evolved from a young artist into a prominent figure in the music industry, continuously pushing creative boundaries and resonating deeply with audiences worldwide.

Songwriting Process

Tate McRae's songwriting process is deeply personal and intuitive. She often starts with raw emotions or experiences, translating them into lyrics and melodies.

Collaborating with producers, she refines these ideas, experimenting with different sounds. This approach ensures her music remains authentic and relatable, reflecting her true self.

Breakthrough Hits

Tate McRae's breakthrough hits, like "you broke me first" and "r u ok," catapulted her into the spotlight with their candid lyrics and catchy melodies. These songs resonated deeply with listeners, showcasing her unique voice and emotional depth.

Their success solidified her place in the music industry and set the stage for her continued rise.

Collaborations and Features

Tate McRae's collaborations and features highlight her versatility and ability to blend seamlessly with other artists. Working with prominent musicians and producers, she explores new sounds and styles, enriching her own music while contributing her unique voice to theirs.

These partnerships not only expand her musical range but also introduce her to diverse audiences, further establishing her presence in the industry.

Live Performances and Tours

Tate McRae's live performances and tours have showcased her dynamic stage presence and vocal prowess. Known for her engaging shows, she connects deeply with audiences through powerful renditions of her hits. Her tours, such as the "i used to think i could fly" tour, highlight her growth as an artist and offer fans an electrifying experience. Each performance is a testament to her evolving artistry and connection with her audience.

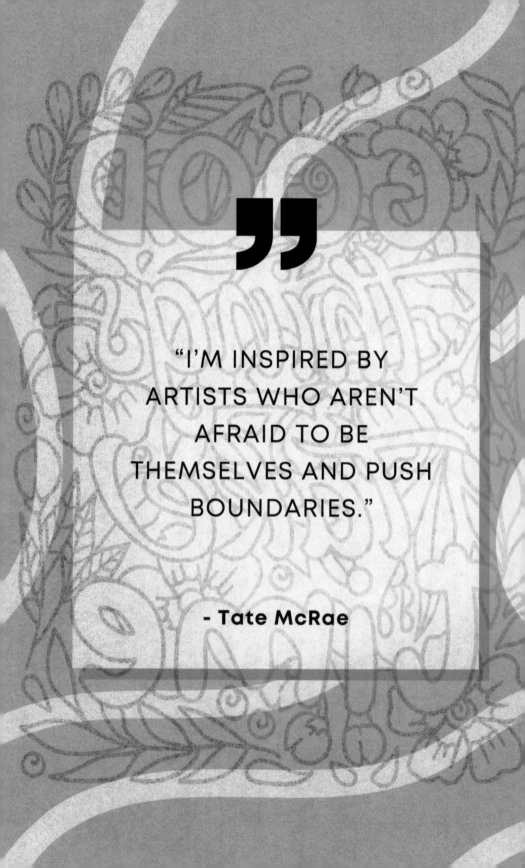

"I'M INSPIRED BY
ARTISTS WHO AREN'T
AFRAID TO BE
THEMSELVES AND PUSH
BOUNDARIES."

- Tate McRae

WORD SEARCH

O	I	Q	I	F	C	U	L	T	U	R	E
G	N	I	M	R	A	W	T	R	A	E	H
T	R	U	H	Q	W	H	V	K	E	B	C
D	M	C	H	A	R	M	D	K	D	O	O
G	L	O	B	A	L	I	U	O	N	C	A
N	A	E	D	R	A	T	S	O	A	D	C
N	O	I	T	I	B	M	A	L	R	O	S
N	O	S	T	A	L	G	I	C	G	V	Y
M	S	L	U	Y	E	H	O	P	E	T	S
R	P	F	Q	U	Q	I	C	E	Z	F	I

Nostalgic   Charm   Heartwarming

Star   Look   Culture   Global   Hope

Grande   Ambition

WORD SEARCH

Create Your Own Lyrics: Use Tate McRae's songs as inspiration to write your own lyrics. Channel your thoughts and emotions into creating a song of your own.

Date:

```
E R U T L U C F I O I O
H E A R T W A R M I N G
C B E K V H W O U R T
O O D K D M R A H C M D
A C N O U I L A B O L G
C D A O S T A R D E A N
S O R L A M B I T I O N
Y V G C I G L A T S O N
S T E P O H E Y U L S M
I F Z E C I O U Q E P R
```

Nostalgic   Charm   Heartwarming

Star   Look   Culture   Global   Hope

Grande   Ambition

"PERFORMING
LIVE IS ONE OF MY
FAVORITE PARTS
OF BEING A
MUSICIAN. IT'S
WHERE I FEEL
MOST ALIVE."

- Tate McRae -

"PERFORMING LIVE IS ONE OF MY FAVORITE PARTS OF BEING A MUSICIAN. IT'S WHERE I FEEL MOST ALIVE."

- Tate McRae

Tate McRae's Secret Diary: Imagine you found Tate's secret diary. What do you think she would write about? Write a pretend entry from her diary about one of her exciting adventures.

Date:

_____

_____

_____

_____

_____

_____

_____

_____

_____

_____

_____

_____

_____

"EVERY SONG I WRITE IS A PIECE OF ME, AND I HOPE PEOPLE CAN SEE THAT THROUGH MY MUSIC."

- Tate McRae

Inspirations and Influences: The Artists She Admires

Tate McRae's music is shaped by a range of influential artists who have inspired her from an early age. These influences have molded her distinctive sound and artistic direction. Here's a look at some of the key figures who have left a lasting impact on her career.

Ariana Grande

Tate McRae admires Ariana Grande for her impressive vocal range and pop artistry. Grande's ability to blend powerful singing with emotive lyrics has been a significant influence on McRae's own music. Inspired by Grande's dynamic performances and versatility. McRae has cited her as a key figure in shaping her approach to both singing and songwriting.

Billie Eilish

Tate McRae admires Billie Eilish for her innovative sound and emotional depth. Eilish's genre-defying music and authentic expression have had a profound impact on McRae's own artistry. The raw, introspective quality of Eilish's work inspires McRae's songwriting and vocal delivery, driving her to explore similar themes of vulnerability and personal experience in her own music.

SZA

Tate McRae draws significant inspiration from SZA, admiring her blend of R&B and pop with deeply personal songwriting. SZA's ability to convey complex emotions and experiences through her music has profoundly influenced McRae's approach to writing and performing. The authenticity and versatility in SZA's work resonate with McRae, motivating her to explore similar themes of vulnerability and self-expression in her own songs.

Lorde

Tate McRae finds inspiration in Lorde's distinctive style and poignant lyrics. Lorde's ability to craft introspective and innovative music resonates deeply with McRae. Admiring Lorde's unique approach to pop and her lyrical storytelling, McRae has been influenced by her ability to blend emotion with a fresh sound. This influence is evident in McRae's own music, where she strives to capture similar depth and originality.

Taylor Swift

Tate McRae admires Taylor Swift for her exceptional storytelling and musical evolution. Swift's talent for crafting relatable lyrics and her versatility across genres have deeply influenced McRae. Inspired by Swift's ability to convey personal experiences with authenticity and creativity, McRae integrates similar emotional depth and narrative quality into her own songwriting, aiming to connect with listeners in a comparable, impactful way.

Gratitude Journal: Write down three things you're grateful for today. It could be something related to Tate McRae, like her music making you happy, or something else entirely.

Date:

Gratitude Journal: Write down three
things you're grateful for today. It
could be something related to Tate
McRae, like her music making you
happy, or something else entirely.

Date: _____ ♥

_____

_____

_____

_____

_____

_____

_____

_____

_____

_____

_____

_____

_____

_____

_____

_____

_____

_____

_____

_____

"

"I'M CONSTANTLY GROWING AS AN ARTIST, AND I HOPE MY MUSIC REFLECTS THAT EVOLUTION."

- Tate McRae

"I'M CONSTANTLY GROWING AS AN ARTIST, AND I HOPE MY MUSIC REFLECTS THAT EVOLUTION."

- Tate McRae

Made in United States
Troutdale, OR
05/29/2025

Made in United States
Troutdale, OR
05/29/2025

31761270R00056